Gen~AI~Que
Celebrating Women Across Generations

Introduction:

In this inaugural edition of our magazine, "Gen~AI~Que," we're proud to showcase the transformative power of AI through stunning visual portraits of women from all walks of life. As you flip through these pages, you'll encounter a diverse array of faces, each uniquely beautiful and radiating strength, grace, and authenticity.

Our Mission:

At "Gen~AI~Que," we believe in celebrating the beauty of diversity and embracing the uniqueness of every individual. Through the lens of artificial intelligence, we aim to highlight the inherent beauty of women of all ages, shapes, and backgrounds. Our goal is not to perpetuate unrealistic beauty standards but to celebrate the real women who inspire us every day.

Embracing New Technology:

As we journey into the new age of AI, we want to appreciate and embrace the opportunities it brings for creativity, innovation, and self-expression. Rather than fearing the unknown, let us embrace the possibilities of this new technology to amplify our individuality and celebrate the beauty that exists within each of us.

Behind the Scenes:

It's important to note that while these portraits are created using cutting-edge AI technology, the women you see in these images are not necessarily fictional characters or unattainable ideals. They were created by real women—mothers, daughters, sisters, friends—whose essence has been captured and celebrated through the magic of AI.

<u>**Embracing Authenticity:**</u>

In a world where digitally altered images often dominate the media landscape, we want to emphasize the importance of authenticity and self-acceptance. These AI-generated portraits serve as a reminder that beauty comes in all shapes, sizes, and ages. They are a celebration of the diversity and resilience of women everywhere.

Closing Thoughts:

As you explore this visual journey, we invite you to appreciate the power of AI to amplify our individuality and showcase the beauty that exists within each of us. Let these portraits inspire you to embrace your own unique beauty and celebrate the remarkable women in your life. With "Gen~AI~Que," we hope to spark conversations, challenge perceptions, and redefine beauty standards in a way that empowers and uplifts women of all ages. Thank you for joining us on this journey of discovery and celebration.

Sincerely,

Michelle Lopez Lopez
Creator

Tezza

All Images made with text prompts, Control Lock, Face lock and Photoreal and Realistic to learn more about creating AI Models hit the link on the last page.

Layla

All Images made with text prompts, Control Lock, Face lock and Photoreal and Realistic to learn more about creating AI Models hit the link on the last page.

All Images made with text prompts, Control Lock, Face lock and Photoreal and Realistic to learn more about creating AI Models hit the link on the last page.

All Images made with text prompts, Control Lock, Face lock and Photoreal and Realistic to learn more about creating AI Models hit the link on the last page.

Pita

All Images made with text prompts, Control Lock, Face lock and Photoreal and Realistic to learn more about creating AI Models hit the link on the last page.

Meeka

All Images made with text prompts, Control Lock, Face lock and Photoreal and Realistic to learn more about creating AI Models hit the link on the last page.

Iya

Victoria

All Images made with text prompts, Control Lock, Face lock and Photoreal and Realistic to learn more about creating AI Models hit the link on the last page.

Blake

Zoey

Claire

Joy

Gura

Abigail

Tia

Emma

Gia & Emi

Girlfriends

at the

Beach

BLLOKNJR
RAUEN

PAVGE
CEN TEV

[https: amazon.com/author/LopezLopez](https://amazon.com/author/LopezLopez)

Want to create pictures using AI Model Generator?
School pictures, holiday photos, family photos,
whatever occassion photos. Then tap on the link
below and take the course today!